The Mayfl

MW01674743

July 15, 1620-May 6, 1621 (Volume 5)

Azel Ames

Alpha Editions

This edition published in 2022

ISBN : 9789356897175

Design and Setting By
Alpha Editions
www.alphaedis.com
Email - info@alphaedis.com

As per information held with us this book is in Public Domain.
This book is a reproduction of an important historical work. Alpha Editions uses the best technology to reproduce historical work in the same manner it was first published to preserve its original nature. Any marks or number seen are left intentionally to preserve its true form.

Contents

CHAPTER VII .... - 1 -
CHAPTER VIII .... - 6 -
ETEXT EDITOR'S BOOKMARKS: .... - 26 -

CHAPTER VII

QUARTERS, COOKING, PROVISIONS

Probably no more vexatious problem presented itself for the time being to the "governors" of the two vessels and their "assistants," upon their selection, than the assignment of quarters to the passengers allotted to their respective ships. That these allotments were in a large measure determined by the requirements of the women and children may be considered certain. The difficulties attendant on due recognition of social and official station (far more imperative in that day than this) were in no small degree lessened by the voluntary assignment of themselves, already mentioned, of some of the Leyden chief people to the smaller ship; but in the interests of the general welfare and of harmony, certain of the leaders, both of the Leyden and London contingents, were of necessity provided for in the larger vessel. The allotments to the respective ships made at Southampton, the designation of quarters in the ships themselves, and the final readjustments upon the MAY-FLOWER at Plymouth (England), when the remaining passengers of both ships had been united, were all necessarily determined chiefly with regard to the needs of the women, girls, and babes. Careful analysis of the list shows that there were, requiring this especial consideration, nineteen women, ten young girls, and one infant. Of the other children, none were so young that they might not readily bunk with or near their fathers in any part of the ship in which the latter might be located.

We know enough of the absolute unselfishness and devotion of all the Leyden leaders, whatever their birth or station,—so grandly proven in those terrible days of general sickness and death at New Plymouth,—to be certain that with them, under all circumstances, it was noblesse oblige, and that no self-seeking would actuate them here. It should be remembered that the MAY-FLOWER was primarily a passenger transport, her passengers being her principal freight and occupying the most of the ship, the heavier cargo being chiefly confined to the "hold." As in that day the passenger traffic was, of course, wholly by sailing vessels, they were built with cabin accommodations for it, as to numbers, etc., proportionately much beyond those of the sailing craft of to-day. The testimony of Captain John Smith, "the navigator," as to the passengers of the MAY-FLOWER "lying wet in their cabins," and that of Bradford as to Billington's "cabin between decks," already quoted, is conclusive as to the fact that she had small cabins (the "staterooms" of to-day), intended chiefly, no doubt, for women and children. The advice of Edward Winslow to his friend George Morton, when the latter was about to come to New England in the ANNE, "build your cabins as open as possible," is suggestive of close cabins and their discomforts endured upon the MAY-FLOWER. It also suggests that the chartering-party was expected in those days to control, if not to do, the "fitting up" of the ship for her voyage. In view of the usual "breadth of beam" of ships of her class and tonnage, aft, and the fore and aft length of the poop, it is not unreasonable to suppose that there were not less than four small cabins on either side of the common (open) cabin or saloon (often depicted as the signing-place of the Compact), under the high poop deck. Constructed on the general plan of such rooms or cabins to-day (with four single berths, in tiers of two on either hand), there would be—if the women and girls were conveniently distributed among them—space for all except the Billingtons, who we know had a cabin (as had also doubtless several of the principal men) built between decks. This would also leave an after cabin for the Master, who not infrequently made his quarters, and those of his chief officer, in the "round house," when one existed, especially in a crowded ship.

Cabins and bunks "between decks" would provide for all of the males of the company, while the seamen, both of the crew and (some of) those in the employ of the Pilgrims—like Trevore and Ely—were no doubt housed in the fore castle. Alderton and English seem to have been counted "of the company." The few data we have permit us to confidently assume that some such disposition of the passengers was (necessarily) made, and that but for the leaky decks, the inseparable discomforts of the sea, and those of over crowding, the wives of the Pilgrims (three of whom gave birth to children aboard the ship), and their daughters, were fairly "berthed."

Bradford is authority for the statement that with the "governor" of the ship's company were chosen "two or three assistants . . . to order [regulate] the people by the way [on the passage] and see to the disposition of the provisions," etc. The last-named duty must have been a most difficult and wearisome one. From what has been shown of the poverty of the ship's cooking facilities (especially for so large a company), one must infer that it would be hopeless to expect to cook food in any quantity, except when all conditions favored, and then but slowly and with much difficulty. From the fact that so many would require food at practically the same hours of the day, it is clear that there must have been distribution of food (principally uncooked) to groups or families, who, with the aid of servants (when available), must each have prepared their own meals, cooking as occasion and opportu nity indicated; much after the manner of the steerage passengers in later days, but before those of the great ocean liners. There appears to have been but one cook for the officers and crew of the ship, and his hands were doubtless full with their demands. It is certain that his service to the passengers must have been very slight. That "the cook" is named as one of the ship's crew who died in Plymouth harbor (New England) is all the knowledge we have concerning him.

The use of and dependence upon tea and coffee, now so universal, and at sea so seemingly indispensable, was then unknown, beer supplying their places, and this happily did not have to be prepared with fire. "Strong waters"—Holland gin and to some extent "aqua vitae" (brandy)—were relied upon for the (supposed) maintenance of warmth. Our Pilgrim Fathers were by no means "total abstainers," and sadly bewailed being deprived of their beer when the supply failed. They also made general and habitual (moderate) use of wine and spirits, though they sharply interdicted and promptly punished their abuse.

In the absence of cooking facilities, it became necessary in that day to rely chiefly upon such articles of food as did not require to be prepared by heat, such as biscuit (hard bread), butter, cheese ("Holland cheese" was a chief staple with the Pilgrims), "haberdyne" (or dried salt codfish), smoked herring, smoked ("cured ") ham and bacon, "dried neat's tongues," preserved and "potted" meats (a very limited list in that day), fruits, etc. Mush, oatmeal, pease-puddings, pickled eggs, sausage meats, salt beef and pork, bacon, "spiced beef," such few vegetables as they had (chiefly cabbages, turnips, and onions,—there were no potatoes in that day), etc., could be cooked in quantity, when the weather permitted, and would then be eaten cold.

Except as dried or preserved fruits, vegetables (notably onions), limes, lemon juice, and the free use of vinegar feebly counteracted, their food was distinctively stimulant of scorbutic and tuberculosis disease, which constant exposure to cold and wet and the overcrowded state of the ship could but increase and aggravate. Bradford narrates of one of the crew of the MAY-FLOWER when in Plymouth harbor, as suggestive of the wretched conditions prevalent in the ship, that one of his shipmates, under an agreement to care for him, "got him a little spice and made him a mess of beef, once or twice," and then deserted him.

Josselyn, in his "Two Voyages to New England," gives as the result of the experience and observations had in his voyages, but a few years later, much that is interesting and of exceptional value as to the food and equipment of passengers to, and colonists in, this part of America. It has especial interest, perhaps, for the author and his readers, in the fact that Josselyn's statements were not known until after the data given in these pages had been independently worked out from various sources, and came therefore as a gratifying confirmation of the conclusions already reached.

Josselyn says as to food, as follows:—"The common proportion of victuals for the sea to a mess (being 4 men) is as followeth:—

"2 pieces of Beef of 3 lb. 1/4 apiece. Pork seems to have been inadvertently omitted.

"Four pounds of Bread [ship-bread].

"One pint & 1/2 of Pease.

"Four Gallons of Bear [Beer], with mustard and vinegar for 3 flesh days in the week."

"For four fish days to each mess per day:—

"Two pieces of Codd or Haberdine, making 3 pieces of a fish, i.e. a dried salt cod being divided into three pieces, 2 of those pieces were to be a day's ration for 4 men.

"Four pounds of Bread.

"Three-quarters of a pound of cheese.

"Bear as before."

"Oatmeal per day for 50 men 1 Gallon [dry], and so proportionable for more or fewer."

"Thus you see the ship's provision is Beefe and Porke, Fish, Butter, Cheese, Pease, Pottage, Water-Gruel, Bisket, and six shilling Bear."

"For private fresh provision you may carry with you (in case you or any of yours should be sick at sea):—

"Conserves of Roses, Clove-Gilliflowers, Wormwood, Green-Ginger, Burnt-Wine, English Spirits, Prunes to stew, Raisons of the Sun, Currence [currants], Sugar, Nutmeg, Mace, Cinna mon, Pepper and Ginger, White Bisket, Butter, or 'Captains biscuit,' made with wheat flour or Spanish Rusk, Eggs, Rice, Juice of Lemons, well put up to cure or prevent the Scurvy, Small Skillets, Pipkins, Porringers and small Frying Pans."

Josselyn further gives us an estimate for:—

"Victuals for a whole year to be carried out of England for one man and so for more after this rate." He annexed also their current prices:—

"Eight bushels of Meal [Rye meal probably intended]
Two bushels of Pease at 3/s
Two bushels of Oatmeal at 4s/6d
One Gallon of Aqua Vitae
One Gallon of Oyl
Two Gallons of Vinegar
[No estimate of Beef or Pork, or of vegetables, is included.]
A Hogshead of English Bear
A Hogshead of Irish Bear
A Hogshead of Vinegar

A bushel of Mustard seed
A Kental [Quintal] of fish, Cod or Haberdine, 112 lb."

Edward Window, in his letter to George Morton before mentioned, advising him as to his voyage, says: "Bring juice of lemons and take it fasting. It is of good use."

It is indeed remarkable that, totally unused to any such conditions, wet, cold, poorly fed, overcrowded, storm-tossed, bruised and beaten, anxious, and with no homes to welcome them, exposed to new hardships and dangers on landing, worn and exhausted, any of the MAY-FLOWER'S company survived. It certainly cannot be accounted strange that infectious diseases, once started among them, should have run through their ranks like fire, taking both old and young. Nor is it strange that—though more inured to hardship and the conditions of sea life—with the extreme and unusual exposure of boat service on the New England coast in mid winter, often wading in the icy water and living aboard ship in a highly infected atmosphere, the seamen should have succumbed to disease in almost equal ratio with the colonists. The author is prepared, after careful consideration, to accept and professionally indorse, with few exceptions, the conclusions as to the probable character of the decimating diseases of the passengers and crew of the MAY-FLOWER, so ably and interestingly presented by Dr. Edward E. Cornwall in the "New England Magazine" for February, 1897— From the fact that Edward Thompson, Jasper More, and Master James Chilton died within a month of the arrival at Cape Cod (and while the ship lay in that harbor), and following the axiom of vital statistics that "for each death two are constantly sick," there must have been some little (though not to say general) sickness on the MAY-FLOWER when she arrived at Cape Cod. It would, in view of the hardship of the voyage, have been very remarkable if this had not been the case. It would have been still more remarkable if the ill-conditioned, thin- blooded, town-bred "servants" and apprentices had not suffered first and most. It is significant that eight out of nine of the male "servants" should have died in the first four months. It was impossible that scurvy should not have been prevalent with both passengers and crew.

CHAPTER VIII

THE MAY-FLOWER'S LADING

Beside her human freight of one hundred and thirty or more passengers and crew, the lading of the MAY-FLOWER when she sailed from Plymouth (England), September 6/16, 1620, was considerable and various. If clearing at a custom-house of to-day her manifest would excite no little interest and surprise. Taking no account of the ship's stores and supplies (necessarily large, like her crew, when bound upon such a voyage, when every possible need till her return to her home port must be provided for before sailing), the colonists' goods and chattels were many, their provisions bulky, their ordnance, arms, and stores (in the hold) heavy, and their trading-stock fairly ample. Much of the cargo originally stowed in the SPEEDWELL, a part, as we know, of her company, and a few of her crew were transferred to the MAY-FLOWER at Plymouth, and there can be no doubt that the ship was both crowded and overladen.

It is altogether probable that the crowded condition of her spar and main decks caused the supply of live-stock taken—whether for consumption upon the voyage or for the planters' needs on shore—to be very limited as to both number and variety. It has been matter of surprise to many that no cattle (not even milch-cows) were taken, but if—as is not unlikely—it was at first proposed to take a cow or two (when both ships were to go and larger space was available), this intent was undoubtedly abandoned at Plymouth, England, when it became evident that there would be dearth of room even for passengers, none whatever for cattle or their fodder (a large and prohibitive quantity of the latter being required for so long a voyage), and that the lateness of the season and its probable hardships would endanger the lives of the animals if taken. So far as appears the only domestic live-stock aboard the MAY-FLOWER consisted of goats, swine, poultry, and dogs. It is quite possible that some few sheep, rabbits, and poultry for immediate consumption (these requiring but little forage) may have been shipped, this being customary then as now. It is also probable that some household pets—cats and caged singing-birds, the latter always numerous in both England and Holland—were carried on board by their owners, though no direct evidence of the fact is found. There is ample proof that goats, swine, poultry, and dogs were landed with the colonists at New Plymouth, and it is equally certain that they had at first neither cattle, horses, nor sheep. Of course the she-goats were their sole reliance for milk for some time, whether afloat or ashore, and goat's flesh and pork their only possibilities in the way of fresh meat for many months, save poultry (and game after landing), though we may be sure, in view of the breeding value of their goats, poultry, and swine, few were consumed for food. The "fresh meat" mentioned as placed before Massasoit' on his first visit was probably venison, though possibly kid's meat, pork, or poultry. Of swine and poultry they must have had a pretty fair supply, judging from their rapid increase, though their goats must have been few. They were wholly without beasts of draft or burden (though it seems strange that a few Spanish donkeys or English "jacks" had not been taken along, as being easily kept, hardy, and strong, and quite equal to light ploughing, hauling, carrying, etc.), and their lack was sorely felt. The space they and their forage demanded it was doubtless considered impracticable to spare. The only dogs that appear in evidence are a large mastiff bitch (the only dog of that breed probably seen on these shores since Pring's "bigge dogges" so frightened the Indians' in this region seventeen years before)

> [Captain Martin Pring had at Plymouth, in 1603, two great "mastive dogges" named "Fool" and "Gallant," the former being trained to carry a half-pike in his mouth. "The Indians were more afraid of these dogs than of twenty men." American Magazine of History; Goodwin, Pilgrim Republic, p. 3.]

and a small spaniel, both the property of passengers, though there may have been others not mentioned. Speaking of the venison found in a tree by one of the exploring parties, Winslow says: "We thought it fitter for the dogs than for us," perhaps suggesting by his word "the" their own dogs aboard ship and provision for them. There is an intimation as to the ownership of these two dogs in the facts that on certainly two occasions John Goodman was accompanied by the little spaniel (once when alone), from which it may perhaps be inferred that he was the dog's master; while the big mastiffs presence when only Peter Browne and Goodman were together suggests that Browne was her owner. The goats, swine, rabbits, and poultry were doubtless penned on the spar-deck forward, while possibly some poultry, and any sheep brought for food, may have been temporarily housed—as was a practice with early voyagers—in the (unused) ship's boats, though these appear to have been so few in number and so much in demand that it is doubtful if they were here available as pens. The heavy cargo and most of the lighter was of course stowed in the hold, as the main deck (or "'tween decks") was mostly occupied as quarters for the male passengers, old and young, though the colonists' shallop, a sloop-rigged boat some thirty feet in length, had been "cut down" and stowed "between the decks" for the voyage. A glimpse of the weary life at sea on that long and dreary passage is given in Bradford's remark that "she was much opened with the people's lying in her during the voyage:' This shallop with her equipment, a possible spare skiff or two, the chests, "boxes," and other personal belongings of the passengers, some few cases of goods, some furniture, etc., constituted the only freight for which there could have been room "between decks," most of the space (aft) being occupied by cabins and bunks.

The provisions in use, both by passengers and crew, were probably kept in the lazarette or "runs," in the stern of the ship, which would be unusually capacious in vessels of this model; some—the bulkiest—in the hold under the forward hatch, as the custom was, and to some extent still is. The food supply of the Pilgrims, constituting part of the MAY- FLOWER'S Cargo, included, as appears from authentic sources:—

Breadstuff's, including,—
  Biscuits or ship-bread (in barrels).
  Oatmeal (in barrels or hogsheads).
  Rye meal (in hogsheads).
Butter (in firkins).
Cheese, "Hollands" and English (in boxes).
Eggs, pickled (in tubs).
Fish, "haberdyne" [or salt dried cod] (in boxes).
Smoked herring (in boxes).
Meats, including,—
  Beef, salt, or "corned" (in barrels).
    Dry-salted (in barrels).
    Smoked (in sacks).
    Dried neats'-tongues (in boxes).
  Pork, bacon, smoked (in sacks or boxes).
    Salt [" corned "] (in barrels).
    Hams and shoulders, smoked (in canvas sacks or hogsheads).
Salt (in bags and barrels).
Vegetables, including,—
  Beans (in bags and barrels).
  Cabbages (in sacks and barrels).
  Onions (in sacks).
  Turnips (in sacks).
  Parsnips (in sacks).
  Pease (in barrels), and
Vinegar (in hogsheads), while,—
Beer (in casks), brandy, "aqua vitae" (in pipes), and gin ["Hollands," "strong waters," or "schnapps"] (in pipes) were no small or unimportant part, from any point of view, of the provision supply.

Winslow, in his letter to George Morton advising him as to his preparations for the voyage over, says: "Be careful to have a very good bread-room to keep your biscuit in." This was to keep them from dampness. Winthrop gives us the memorandum of his order for the ship- bread for his voyage in 1630. He says: "Agreed with Keene of Southwark, baker, for 20,000 of Biscuit,

15,000 of brown, and 5,000 of white." Captain Beecher minutes: "10 M. of bread for the ship ARBELLA." Beecher's memorandum of "oatmeal" is "30 bushels." Winslow mentions "oatmeal," and Winthrop notes among the provisions bought by Captain William Pierce, "4 hhds. of oatmeal." Rye meal was usually meant by the term "meal," and Window in his letter to George Morton advises him: "Let your meal be so hard-trod in your casks that you shall need an adz or hatchet to work it out with;" and also to "be careful to come by [be able to get at] some of your meal to spend [use] by the way." Notwithstanding that Bradford' speaks of their "selling away" some "60 firkins of butter," to clear port charges at Southampton, and the leaders, in their letter to the Adventurers from that port (August 3), speak of themselves, when leaving Southampton in August, 1620, as "scarce having any butter," there seems to have been some left to give as a present to Quadrequina, Massasoit's brother, the last of March following, which would indicate its good "keeping" qualities. Wood, in his "New England's Prospect" (ch. 2), says: "Their butter and cheese were corrupted." Bradford mentions that their lunch on the exploration expedition of November 15, on Cape Cod, included "Hollands cheese," which receives also other mention. There is a single mention, in the literature of the day, of eggs preserved in salt, for use on shipboard. "Haberdyne" (or dried salt cod) seems to have been a favorite and staple article of diet aboard ship. Captain Beecher minutes "600 haberdyne for the ship ARBELLA." Wood says: "Their fish was rotten." Smoked "red-herring" were familiar food to all the MAY-FLOWER company. No house or ship of England or Holland in that day but made great dependence upon them. Bacon was, of course, a main staple at sea. In its half-cooked state as it came from the smoke-house it was much relished with their biscuit by seamen and others wishing strong food, and when fried it became a desirable article of food to all except the sick. Mention is made of it by several of the early Pilgrim writers. Carlyle, as quoted, speaks of it as a diet-staple on the MAY-FLOWER. Salt ("corned") beef has always been a main article of food with seamen everywhere. Wood' states that the "beef" of the Pilgrims was "tainted." In some way it was made the basis of a reputedly palatable preparation called "spiced beef," mentioned as prepared by one of the sailors for a shipmate dying on the MAY-FLOWER in Plymouth harbor. It must have been a very different article from that we now find so acceptable under that name in England. Winthrop' gives the price of his beef at "19 shillings per cwt." Winslow advises his friend Morton, in the letter so often quoted, not to have his beef "dry-salted," saying, "none can do it better than the sailors," which is a suggestion not readily understood. "Smoked" beef was practically the same as that known as "jerked," "smoked," or "dried" beef in America. A "dried neat's- tongue" is named as a contribution of the Pilgrims to the dinner for Captain Jones and his men on February 21, 1621, when they had helped to draw up and mount the cannon upon the platform on the hill at Plymouth. Winthrop paid "14d. a piece" for his "neats' tongues." The pork of the Pilgrims is also said by Wood' to have been "tainted." Winthrop states that his pork cost "20 pence the stone" (14 lbs.).

Hams seem to have been then, as now, a highly-prized article of diet. Goodwin mentions that the salt used by the Pilgrims was (evaporated) "sea-salt" and very "impure." Winthrop mentions among his supplies, "White, Spanish, and Bay salt."

The beans of the Pilgrims were probably of the variety then known as "Spanish beans." The cabbages were apparently boiled with meat, as nowadays, and also used considerably for "sour-krout" and for pickling, with which the Leyden people had doubtless become familiar during their residence among the Dutch. As anti-scorbutics they were of much value. The same was true of onions, whether pickled, salted, raw, or boiled. Turnips and parsnips find frequent mention in the early literature of the first settlers, and were among their stock vegetables. Pease were evidently staple articles of food with the Plymouth people, and are frequently named. They probably were chiefly used for porridge and puddings, and were used in large quantities, both afloat and ashore.

Vinegar in hogsheads was named on the food-list of every ship of the Pilgrim era. It was one of their best antiscorbutics, and was of course a prime factor in their use of "sour krout," pickling, etc. The fruits, natural, dried, and preserved, were probably, in that day, in rather small supply. Apples, limes, lemons, prunes, olives, rice, etc., were among the luxuries of a voyage, while dried or preserved fruits and small fruits were not yet in common use. Winslow, in the letter cited, urges that "your casks for beer . . . be iron bound, at least for the first [end] tyre" [hoop]. Cushman states that they had ample supplies of beer offered them both in Kent and Amsterdam. The planters' supply seems to have failed, however, soon after the company landed, and they were obliged to rely upon the whim of the Captain of the MAY-FLOWER for their needs, the ship's supply being apparently separate from that of the planters, and lasting longer. Winthrop's supply seems to have been large ("42 tons"—probably tuns intended). It was evidently a stipulation of the charter-party that the ship should, in part at least, provision her crew for the voyage,—certainly furnish their beer. This is rendered certain by Bradford's difficulty (as stated by himself) with Captain Jones, previously referred to, showing that the ship had her own supply of beer, separate from that of the colonists, and that it was intended for the seamen as well as the officers.

Bradford mentions "aqua vitae" as a constituent of their lunch on the exploring party of November 15. "Strong waters" (or Holland gin) are mentioned as a part of the entertainment given Massasoit on his first visit, and they find frequent mention otherwise. Wine finds no mention. Bradford states in terms: "Neither ever had they any supply of foode from them [the Adventurers] but what they first brought with them;" and again, "They never had any supply of vitales more afterwards (but what the Lord gave them otherwise), for all ye company [the Adventurers] sent at any time was allways too short for those people yt came with it."

The clothing supplies of the Pilgrims included hats, caps, shirts, neck- cloths, jerkins, doublets, waistcoats, breeches (stuff and leather), "hosen," stockings, shoes, boots, belts (girdles), cloth, piece-goods (dress-stuff's), "haberdasherie," etc., etc., all of which, with minor items for men's and women's use, find mention in their early narratives, accounts, and correspondence. By the will of Mr. Mullens it appears that he had twenty-one dozen of shoes and thirteen pairs of boots on board, doubtless intended as medium of exchange or barter. By the terms of the. contract with the colonists, the Merchant Adventurers were to supply all their actual necessities of Clothing food, clothing, etc., for the full term of seven years, during which the labors of the "planters" were to be for the joint account. Whether under this agreement they were bound to fully "outfit" the colonists before they embarked (and did so), as was done by Higginson's company coming to Salem in 1628-29 at considerable cost per capita, and as was done for those of the Leyden people who came over in 1629 with Pierce in the MAY-FLOWER and the TALBOT to Salem, and again in 1630 with the same Master (Pierce) in the LION by the Plymouth successors to the Adventurers (without recompense), does not clearly appear. No mention is found of any "outfitting" of the MAY-FLOWER passengers except the London apprentices. There is no doubt that a considerable supply of all the above-named articles was necessarily sent by the Adventurers on the MAY-FLOWER, both for the Pilgrims' needs on the voyage and in the new colony, as also for trading purposes. There seems to have been at all times a supreme anxiety, on the part of both Pilgrim and Puritan settlers, to get English clothes upon their red brethren of the forest, whether as a means of exchange for peltry, or for decency's sake, is not quite clear. There was apparently a greater disparity in character, intelligence, and station between the leaders of Higginson's and Winthrop's companies and their followers than between the chief men of the Pilgrims and their associates. With the former were titles and considerable representation of wealth and position. With the passengers of the MAY-FLOWER a far greater equality in rank, means, intelligence, capacity, and character was noticeable. This was due in part, doubtless, to the religious beliefs and training of the Leyden contingent, and had prompt illustration in their Compact, in which all stood at once on an equal footing. There was but little of the "paternal" nature in the form of their government (though something at times in their punishments), and there was much personal dignity and independence of the indi vidual. An equipment having so much of the character of a uniform—not to say "livery "—as that furnished by Higginson's company to its people suggests the "hedger and ditcher" type of colonists (of whom there were very few among the Plymouth settlers), rather than the scholar, publisher, tradesman, physician, hatter, smith, carpenter, "lay reader," and soldier of the Pilgrims, and would certainly have been obnoxious to their finer sense of personal dignity and proportion. Doubtless an equivalent provision existed—though in less "all-of-a-pattern " character—in the bales and boxes of the MAY-FLOWER'S cargo for every need suggested by the list of the Higginson "outfit," which is given herewith, both as matter of interest and as affording an excellent idea of the accepted style and needs in dress of a New England settler (at least of the men) of 1620-30. One cannot fail to wonder at the noticeably infrequent mention of provision in apparel, etc., for the women and children. The inventory of the "Apparell for 100 men" furnished by Higginson's company in 1628-29 gives us, among others, the following items of clothing for each emigrant:— 4 "peares of shoes." 4 "peares of stockings." 1 "peare Norwich gaiters." 4 "shirts." 2 "suits dublet and hose of leather lyn'd with oyld skyn leather, ye hose & dublett with hooks & eyes." 1 "sute of Norden dussens or hampshire kersies lynd the hose with skins, dublets with lynen of gilford or gedlyman kerseys." 4 bands. 2 handkerchiefs. 1 "wastecoat of greene cotton bound about with red tape." 1 leather girdle. 1 "Monmouth cap." 1 "black hatt lyned in the brows with lether." 5 "Red knitt capps milf'd about 5d apiece." 2 "peares of gloves." 1 "Mandiliion lynd with cotton" [mantle or greatcoat]. 1 "peare of breeches and waistcoat." 1 "leather sute of Dublett & breeches of oyled leather." 1 "peare of leather breeches and drawers to weare with both there other sutes."

In 1628 Josselyn put the average cost of clothing to emigrants to New England at L4 each. In 1629 good shoes cost the "Bay" colonists 2s/7d per pair. In his "Two Voyages to New England "previously referred to, Josselyn gives an estimate (made about 1628) of the "outfit" in clothing needed by a New England settler of his time. He names as "Apparel for one man—and after this rate for more:—"

One Hatt
One Monmouth Cap
Three falling bands
Three Shirts
One Wastcoat
One Suite of Frize (Frieze)
One Suite of Cloth
One Suite of Canvas
Three Pairs of Irish Stockings
Four Pairs of Shoes
One Pair of Canvas Sheets

Seven ells of coarse canvas, to make a bed at sea for two men,
to be filled with straw
One Coarse Rug at Sea

The Furniture of the Pilgrims has naturally been matter of much interest to their descendants and others for many years. While it is doubtful if a single article now in existence can be positively identified and truthfully certified as having made the memorable voyage in the MAY- FLOWER (nearly everything having, of course, gone to decay with the wear and tear of more than two hundred and fifty years), this honorable origin is still assigned to many heirlooms, to some probably correctly. Dr. Oliver Wendell Holmes in his delightful lines, "On Lending a Punch Bowl," humorously claims for his convivial silver vessel a place with the Pilgrims:—

"Along with all the furniture, to fill their new abodes,
To judge by what is still on hand, at least a hundred loads."

To a very few time-worn and venerated relics—such as Brewster's chair and one or more books, Myles Standish's Plymouth sword, the Peregrine White cradle, Winslow's pewter, and one or two of Bradford's books—a strong probability attaches that they were in veritate, as traditionally avowed, part of the MAY-FLOWER'S freight, but of even these the fact cannot be proven beyond the possibility of a doubt.

From its pattern and workmanship, which are of a period antedating the "departure from Delfshaven," and the ancient tradition which is traceable to Brewster's time, it appears altogether probable that what is known as "Elder Brewster's chair" came with him on the ship. There is even greater probability as to one of his books bearing his autograph.

The sword of Myles Standish, in possession of the Pilgrim Society, may claim, with equal probability, MAY-FLOWER relation, from its evident antiquity and the facts that, as a soldier, his trusty blade doubtless stayed with him, and that it is directly traceable in his descendants' hands, back to his time; but an equally positive claim is made for similar honors for another sword said to have also belonged to the Captain, now in the keeping of the Massachusetts Historical Society.

The Peregrine White cradle "is strongly indorsed as of the MAY-FLOWER, from the facts that it is, indubitably, of a very early Dutch pattern and manufacture; that Mrs. White was anticipating the early need of a cradle when leaving Holland; and that the descent of this one as an heirloom in her (second) family is so fairly traced."

The pewter and the silver flask of Winslow not only bear very early "Hallmarks," but also the arms of his family, which it is not likely he would have had engraved on what he may have bought after notably becoming the defender of the simplicity and democracy of the "Pilgrim Republic." Long traceable use in his family strengthens belief in the supposition that these articles came with the Pilgrims, and were then very probably heirlooms. One of Governor Bradford's books (Pastor John Robinson's "Justification of Separation"), published in 1610, and containing the Governor's autograph, bears almost 'prima facie' evidence of having come with him in the MAY-FLOWER, but of course might, like the above-named relics, have come in some later ship.

In this connection it is of interest to note what freight the MAY-FLOWER carried for the intellectual needs of the Pilgrims. Of Bibles, as the "book of books," we may be sure—even without the evidence of the inventories of the early dead—there was no lack, and there is reason to believe that they existed in several tongues, viz. in English, Dutch, and possibly French (the Walloon contribution from the Huguenots), while there is little doubt that, alike as publishers and as "students of the Word," Brewster, Bradford, and Winslow, at least, were possessed of, and more or less familiar with, both the Latin and Greek Testaments. It is altogether probable, however, that Governor Bradford's well attested study of "the oracles of God in the original" Hebrew, and his possession of the essential Hebrew Bible, grammar, and lexicon, were of a later day. Some few copies of the earliest hymnals ("psalme-bookes")—then very limited in number—there is evidence that the Holland voyagers had with them in the singing of their parting hymns at Leyden and Delfshaven, as mentioned by Winslow and in the earlier inventories: These metrical versions of the Psalms constituted at the time, practically, the only hymnology permitted in the worship of the "Separatists," though the grand hymn of Luther, "Ein feste Burg ist unser Gott," doubtless familiar to them, must have commended itself as especially comforting and apposite.

Of the doctrinal tracts of their beloved Pastor, John Robinson, there is every probability, as well as some proof, that there was good supply, as well as those of Ainsworth and Clyfton and of the works of William Ames, the renowned Franeker Professor, the controversial opponent but sincere friend of Robinson: the founder of evangelical "systematic theology," [method—Methodist? D.W.] whom death alone prevented from becoming the President of Harvard College. We may be equally sure that the few cases of books in the freight of the Pilgrim ship included copies of the publications of the "hidden and hunted press" of Brewster and Brewer, and some at least of the issues of their fellows in tribulation at Amsterdam and in Scotland and England. Some few heavy tomes and early classics in English, Dutch, Latin, and Greek were also presumably among the goodly number of books brought in the MAY FLOWER by Brewster, Bradford, Winslow, Fuller, Hopkins, Allerton, Standish, and others, though it is probable that the larger part of the very considerable library of four hundred volumes, left at his death by Brewster (including sixty-two in Latin), and of the respectable libraries of Fuller, Standish, and others, named in their respective inventories, either were brought over in the later ships, or were the products of the earliest printers of New England. One is surprised and amused that the library of the good Dr. Fuller should contain so relatively small a proportion of medical works (although the number in print prior to his death in 1633 was not great), while rich in religious works pertinent to his functions as deacon. It is equally interesting to note that the inventory of the soldier Standish should name only one book on military science, "Bariffe's Artillery," though it includes abundant evidence to controvert, beyond reasonable doubt, the suggestion which has been made, that he was of the Romanist faith. Just which of the books left by the worthies named, and others whose inventories we possess, came with them in the Pilgrim ship, cannot be certainly determined, though, as before noted, some still in existence bear intrinsic testimony that they were of the number. There is evidence that Allerton made gift of a book to Giles Heale of the MAY-FLOWER (perhaps the ship's surgeon), while the ship lay at Plymouth, and Francis Cooke's inventory includes "1 great Bible and 4 olde bookes," which as they were "olde," and he was clearly not a book-buyer, very probably came with him in the ship. In fact, hardly an adult of the Leyden colonists, the inventory of whose estate at death we possess, but left one or more books which may have been his companions on the voyage.

Some of the early forms of British and Dutch calendars, "annuals," and agricultural "hand-books," it is certain were brought over by several families, and were doubtless much consulted and well-thumbed "guides, counsellors, and friends" in the households of their possessors. The great preponderance of reading matter brought by the little colony was, however, unquestionably of the religious controversial order, which had been so much a part of their lives, and its sum total was considerable. There are intimations, in the inventories of the Fathers, of a few works of historical cast, but of these not many had yet been printed. "Caesar's Commentaries," a "History of the World," and a "History of Turkey" on Standish's shelves, with the two Dictionaries and "Peter Martyr on Rome" on Dr. Fuller's, were as likely to have come in the first ship, and to have afforded as much satisfaction to the hungry readers of the little community as any of the books we find named in the lists of their little stock. It is pathetic to note, in these days of utmost prodigality in juvenile literature, that for the Pilgrim children, aside from the "Bible stories," some of the wonderful and mirth-provoking metrical renderings of the "Psalme booke," and the "horne booke," or primer (the alphabet and certain elementary contributions in verse or prose, placed between thin covers of transparent horn for protection), there was almost absolutely nothing in the meagre book-freight of the Pilgrim ark. "Milk for

Babes," whether as physical or mental pabulum, was in poor supply aboard the MAY-FLOWER.

The most that can be claimed with confidence, for particular objects of alleged MAY-FLOWER relation, is that there is logical and moral certainty that there was a supply of just such things on board, because they were indispensable, and because every known circumstance and condition indicates their presence in the hands to which they are assigned, while tradition and collateral evidence confirm the inference and sometimes go very far to establish their alleged identity, and their presence with their respective owners upon the ship. A few other articles besides those enumerated in possession of the Pilgrim Society, and of other societies and individuals, present almost equally strong claims with those named, to be counted as "of MAY-FLOWER belonging," but in no case is the connection entirely beyond question. Where so competent, interested, and conscientious students of Pilgrim history as Hon. William T. Davis, of Plymouth, and the late Dr. Thomas B. Drew, so long the curator of the Pilgrim Society, cannot find warrant for a positive claim in behalf of any article as having come, beyond a doubt, "in the MAY FLOWER," others may well hesitate to insist upon that which, however probable and desirable, is not susceptible of conclusive proof.

That certain articles of household furniture, whether now existent or not, were included in the ship's cargo, is attested by the inventories of the small estates of those first deceased, and, by mention or implication, in the narratives of Bradford, Winslow, Morton, and other contemporaries, as were also many utensils and articles of domestic use. There were also beyond question many not so mentioned, which may be safely named as having very certainly been comprised in the ship's lading, either because in themselves indispensable to the colonists, or because from the evidence in hand we know them to have been inseparable from the character, social status, daily habits, home life, or ascertained deeds of the Pilgrims. When it is remembered that furnishings, however simple, were speedily required for no less than nineteen "cottages" and their households, the sum total called for was not inconsiderable.

> [Bradford, in Mourt's Relation (p. 68), shows that the colonists were divided up into "nineteen families," that "so we might build fewer houses." Winslow, writing to George Morton, December 11/21, 1621, says: "We have built seven dwelling-houses and four for the use of the plantation." Bradford (Historie, Mass. ed. p. 110) calls the houses "small cottages."]

Among the furniture for these "cottages" brought on the Pilgrim ship may be enumerated: chairs, table-chairs, stools and forms (benches), tables of several sizes and shapes (mostly small), table-boards and "cloathes," trestles, beds; bedding and bed-clothing, cradles, "buffets," cupboards and "cabinets," chests and chests of drawers, boxes of several kinds and "trunks," andirons, "iron dogs," "cob-irons," fire-tongs and "slices" (shovels), cushions, rugs, and "blanckets," spinning wheels, hand-looms, etc., etc. Among household utensils were "spits," "bake-kettles," pots and kettles (iron, brass, and copper), frying-pans, "mortars" and pestles (iron, brass, and "belle-mettle"), sconces, lamps (oil "bettys"), candlesticks, snuffers, buckets, tubs, "runlets," pails and baskets, "steel yards," measures, hour-glasses and sun-dials, pewter-ware (platters, plates, mugs, porringers, etc.), wooden trenchers, trays, "noggins," "bottles," cups, and "lossets." Earthen ware, "fatten" ware (mugs, "jugs," and "crocks "), leather ware (bottles, "noggins," and cups), table-ware (salt "sellars," spoons, knives, etc), etc. All of the foregoing, with numerous lesser articles, have received mention in the early literature of the Pilgrim exodus, and were undeniably part of the MAY-FLOWER'S lading.

The MAY-FLOWER origin claimed for the "Governor Carver chair" and the "Elder Brewster chair" rests wholly upon tradition, and upon the venerable pattern and aspect of the chairs themselves. The "Winslow chair," in possession of the Pilgrim Society at Plymouth (Mass.), though bearing evidence of having been "made in Cheapside, London, in 1614," is not positively known to have been brought on the MAY-FLOWER. Thacher's "History of Plymouth" (p. 144.) states that "a sitting-chair, said to have been screwed to the floor of the MAY-FLOWER'S cabin for the convenience of a lady, is known to have been in the possession of Penelope Winslow (who married James Warren), and is now in possession of Hannah White." There are certain venerable chairs alleged, with some show of probability, to have been the property of Captain Standish, now owned in Bridgewater, but there is no record attached to them, and they are not surely assignable to either ship or owner. That some few tables —mostly small—were brought in the MAY-FLOWER, there is some evidence, but the indications are that what were known as "table-boards"—long and narrow boards covered with what were called "board-cloths"—very largely took the place of tables. The walnut-top table, said to have once been Governor Winslow's and now in possession of the Pilgrim Society, is not known to have come over with him, and probably did not. It was very likely bought for the use of the Council when he was governor. The "table-boards" mentioned were laid on "trestles" (cross-legged and folding supports of proper height), which had the great merit that they could be placed in any convenient spot and as easily folded up, and with the board put away, leaving the space which a table would have permanently occupied free for other use.

Bradford mentions that when the fire of Sunday, January 14., 1621, occurred in the "common house," the "house was as full of beds as they could lie one by another." There is a doubt, however, whether this indicates bedsteads or (probably) "pallets" only. Beds, bedding of all sorts, pillow-"beers," pillow-cases and even "mattrises," are of most frequent mention in the earliest wills and inventories. (See Appendix.) "Buffets," "cupboards," and "cabinets," all find mention in the earliest writers and inventories, and one or two specimens, for which a MAY-FLOWER history is claimed, are in possession of the Pilgrim Society and others. The "White" cabinet, of putative MAY-FLOWER connection, owned by the Pilgrim Society, is a fine example of its class, and both its "ear marks" and its known history support the probable truth of the claim made for it. Of "chests" and "chests-of-drawers" there were doubtless goodly numbers in the ship, but with the exception of a few chests (or the fragments of them), for which a MAY-FLOWER passage is vaunted, little is known of them. The chest claimed to be that of Elder Brewster, owned by the Connecticut Historical Society, was not improb ably his, but that it had any MAY-FLOWER relation is not shown. A fragment of a chest claimed to have been "brought by Edward Winslow in the MAY-FLOWER" is owned by the Pilgrim Society, and bears considerable evidence of the probable validity of such claim, but proof positive is lacking. Boxes of several kinds and sizes were part of the Pilgrims' chattels on their ship, some of them taking the place of the travellers' "trunks" of to-day, though "trunks" were then known by that name and find early mention in Pilgrim inventories, and there were no doubt some upon the Pilgrim ship. A few claiming such distinction are exhibited, but without attested records of their origin.

"Andirons, fire-dogs, and cob-irons" (the latter to rest roasting spits upon) were enumerated among the effects of those early deceased among the Pilgrims, rendering it well-certain that they must have been part of their belongings on the MAY-FLOWER. Fire-tongs and "slices" [shovels] are also frequently mentioned in early Pilgrim inventories, placing them in the same category with the "andirons and fire-dogs."

In "Mourt's Relation," in the accounts given of the state reception of Massasoit, "a green rug and three or four cushions" are shown to have performed their parts in the official ceremonies, and were, of course, necessarily brought in the MAY-FLOWER.

Spinning-wheels and hand-looms were such absolute necessities, and were so familiar and omnipresent features of the lives and labors of the Pilgrim housewives and their Dutch neighbors of Leyden, that we should be certain that they came with the Pilgrims, even if they did not find mention in the earliest Pilgrim inventories. Many ancient ones are exhibited in the "Old Colony," but it is not known that it is claimed for any of them that they came in the first ship. It is probable that some of the "cheese fatts" and churns so often named in early inventories came in the ship, though at first there was, in the absence of milch kine, no such use for them as there had been in both England and Holland, and soon was in New England.

Among cooking utensils the roasting "spit" was, in one form or another, among the earliest devices for cooking flesh, and as such was an essential of every household. Those brought by the Plymouth settlers were probably, as indicated by the oldest specimens that remain to us, of a pretty primitive type. The ancient "bake-kettle" (sometimes called "pan"), made to bury in the ashes and thus to heat above and below, has never been superseded where resort must be had to the open fire for cooking, and (practically unchanged) is in use to-day at many a sheep- herder's and cowboy's camp fire of the Far West. We may be sure that it was in every MAY-FLOWER family, and occasional ancient specimens are yet to be found in "Old Colony" garrets. Pots and kettles of all sorts find more frequent mention in the early inventories than anything else, except muskets and swords, and were probably more numerous upon the ship than any other cooking utensil. A few claimed to be from the Pilgrim ship are exhibited, chief of which is a large iron pot, said to have been "brought by Myles Standish in the MAY-FLOWER," now owned by the Pilgrim Society.

Hardly an early Pilgrim inventory but includes "a mortar and pestle," sometimes of iron, sometimes of "brass" or "belle-mettle" (bell metal). They were of course, in the absence of mills, and for some purposes for which small hand mills were not adapted, prime necessities, and every house hold had one. A very fine one of brass (with an iron pestle), nine and a half inches across its bell-shaped top,—exhibited by the Pilgrim Society, and said to have been "brought in the MAY-FLOWER by Edward Winslow,"—seems to the author as likely to have been so as almost any article for which that distinction is claimed.

The lighting facilities of the Pilgrims were fewer and cruder than those for cooking. They possessed the lamp of the ancient Romans, Greeks, and Hebrews, with but few improvements,—a more or less fanciful vessel for oil, with a protuberant nose for a wick, and a loose-twisted cotton wick. Hand-lamps of this general form and of various devices, called "betty- lamps," were commonly used, with candlesticks of various metals,—iron, brass, silver, and copper,—though but few of any other ware. For wall- lighting two or more candle sockets were brought together in "sconces," which were more or less elaborate in design and finish. One of the early writers (Higginson) mentions the abundance of oil (from fish) available for lamps, but all tallow and suet used by the early colonists was, for some years (till cattle became plentiful), necessarily imported. Some of the "candle-snuffers" of the "first comers" doubtless still remain. We may be sure every family had its candles, "betty-lamps," candlesticks, and "snuffers." "Lanthorns" were of the primitive, perforated tin variety—only "serving to make darkness visible" now found in a few old attics in Pilgrim towns, and on the "bull-carts" of the peons of Porto Rico, by night. Fire, for any purpose, was chiefly procured by the use of flint, steel, and tinder, of which many very early specimens exist. Buckets, tubs, and pails were, beyond question, numerous aboard the ship, and were among the most essential and highly valued of Pilgrim utensils. Most, if not all of them, we may confidently assert, were brought into requisition on that Monday "wash-day" at Cape Cod, the first week-day after their arrival, when the women went ashore to do their long- neglected laundrying, in the comparatively fresh water of the beach pond at Cape Cod harbor. They are frequently named in the earliest inventories. Bradford also mentions the filling of a "runlet" with water at the Cape. The "steel-yards" and "measures" were the only determiners of weight and quantity—as the hour-glass and sun dial were of time— possessed at first (so far as appears) by the passengers of the Pilgrim ship, though it is barely possible that a Dutch clock or two may have been among the possessions of the wealthiest. Clocks and watches were not yet in common use (though the former were known in England from 1540), and except that in "Mourt's Relation" and Bradford's "Historie" mention is made of the time of day as such "o'clock" (indicating some degree of familiarity with clocks), no mention is made of their possession at the first. Certain of the leaders were apparently acquainted at Leyden with the astronomer Galileo, co-resident with them there, and through this acquaintance some of the wealthier and more scholarly may have come to know, and even to own, one of the earliest Dutch clocks made with the pendulum invented by Galileo, though hardly probable as early as 1620. Pocket watches were yet practically unknown.

Except for a few pieces of silver owned by the wealthiest of their number, pewter was the most elegant and expensive of the Pilgrims' table- ware. A pewter platter said to have been "brought over in the MAY- FLOWER" is now owned by the Pilgrim Society, which also exhibits smaller pewter formerly Edward Winslow's, and bearing his "arms," for which, as previously noted, a like claim is made. Platters, dishes, "potts," ladles, bottles, "flaggons," "skelletts," cups, porringers, "basons," spoons, candlesticks, and salt "sellars," were among the many pewter utensils unmistakably brought on the good ship.

The wooden-ware of the colonists, brought with them, was considerable and various. The Dutch were long famous for its fabrication. There was but very little china, glass, or pottery of any kind in common use in western Europe in 1620; some kinds were not yet made, and pewter, wood, and leather largely filled their places. Wooden trenchers (taking the place of plates), trays, "noggins" (jug or pitcher- like cups), cups, and "lossets" (flat dishes like the bread-plates of to day), were of course part of every housewife's providings.

Some few of Pilgrim origin possibly still exist. As neither coffee, tea, nor china had come into use, the cups and saucers which another century brought in —to delight their owners in that day and the ceramic hunter in this— were not among the "breakables" of the "good-wife" of the MAY-FLOWER. The "table-plenishings" had not much variety, but in the aggregate the (first) "nineteen families" must have required quite a quantity of spoons, knives, salt "sellars," etc. Forks there were none, and of the accessories of to-day (except napkins), very few. Meat was held by the napkin while being cut with the knife. Josselyn' gives a list of "Implements for a family of six persons" going to New England.

Kitchen utensils:—

"1 Iron Pot.
1 Great Copper Kettle.
1 Small Kettle.
1 Lesser Kettle.
1 Large Frying pan.
1 Brass Mortar.
1 Spit.
1 Gridiron.
2 Skillets.
Platters, dishes, and spoons of wood.
A pair of Bellows.
A Skoope, etc."

Among the implements of husbandry, etc., and mechanics' tools we find evidence of hoes, spades, shovels, scythes, "sikles," mattocks, bill- hooks, garden-rakes, hay-forks ("pitch-forks"), besides seed-grain and garden seeds. Axes, saws, hammers, "adzs," augers, chisels, gouges, squares, hatchets, an "iron jack-scrue," "holdfasts" (vises), blacksmiths' tools, coopers' tools, iron and steel in bar, anvils, chains, etc., "staples and locks," rope, lime (for mortar), nails, etc., are also known to have been in the ship. Francis Eaton, the carpenter, seems to have had a very respectable "kit," and Fletcher, the smith, was evidently fairly "outfitted."

The implements of husbandry were of the lighter (?) sort; no ploughs, harrows, carts, harness, stone-drags, or other farming tools requiring the strength of beasts for their use, were included. In nothing could they have experienced so sharp a contrast as in the absence of horses, cattle, and sheep in their husbandry, and especially of milch kine. Bradford and Window both mention hoes, spades, mattocks, and sickles, while shovels, scythes, bill-hooks (brush-scythes, the terrible weapons of the English peasantry in their great "Mon mouth" and earlier uprisings), pitchforks, etc., find very early mention in inventories and colonial records. Josselyn, in his "Two Voyages to New England," gives, in 1628, the following very pertinent list of "Tools for a Family of six persons, and so after this rate for more,—intending for New England." This may be taken as fairly approximating the possessions of the average MAY-FLOWER planter, though probably somewhat exceeding individual supplies. Eight years of the Pilgrims' experience had taught those who came after them very much that was of service.

5 Broad Howes [hoes]. 6 Chisels. 5 Narrow Howes [hoes]. 3 Gimblets. 5 Felling Axes. 2 hatchets. 2 steel hand saws. 2 frones (?) to cleave pail! (Probably knives for cleaving pail stock.) 2 hand saws. 2 hand-bills. 1 whip saw, set and files with box. Nails of all sorts. 2 Pick-axes. A file and rest. 3 Locks and 3 paire fetters. 2 Hammers. 2 Currie Combs. 3 Shovels. Brands for beasts. 2 Spades. A hand vice. 2 Augers. A pitchfork, etc. 2 Broad Axes.

Unhappily we know little from contemporaneous authority as to what grain and other seeds the Pilgrims brought with them for planting. We may be sure, however, that rye, barley, oats, wheat, pease, and beans were the bulkiest of this part of their freight, though Bradford mentions the planting of "garden seeds" their first spring.

While we know from the earliest Pilgrim chronicles that their mechanics' implements embraced axes, saws, hammers, "adzs," augers, hatchets, an "iron jack-scrue," "staples and locks," etc., we know there must have been many other tools not mentioned by them, brought over with the settlers. The "great iron-scrue," as Bradford calls it in his original MS., played, as all know, a most important part on the voyage, in forcing the "cracked and bowed" deck-beam of the ship into place. Governor Bradford tells us that "it was brought on board by one of the Leyden passengers," and one may hazard the guess that it was by either Moses Fletcher, the smith, or Francis Eaton, the "carpenter." "Staples" and "locks" found their place and mention, as well as the "chains," "manacles," and "leg-irons" named in the list of accoutrements for offence or defence, when it became necessary to chain up the Indian spy of the Neponsets (as narrated by Winslow in his "Good Newes from New England") and other evil-doers. The planters seem to have made stiff "mortar," which premises the use of lime and indicates a supply.

Among the fishing and fowling implements of the MAY FLOWER colonists are recorded, nets, "seynes," twine, fish hooks, muskets (for large game), "fowling pieces," powder, "goose-shot," "hail-shot," etc.

Such early mention is found of the nets, "seynes," etc., of their fishing equipment, as to leave no room for doubt that store of them was brought in the ship. They seem to have been unfortunate in the size of their fish-hooks, which are spoken of as "too large" even for cod. They must, as Goodwin remarks, "have been very large." Window also says, "We wanted fit and strong seines and other netting."

They seem to have relied upon their muskets to some extent for wild fowl (as witness Winslow's long and successful shot at a duck, on his visit to Massasoit), as they undoubtedly did for deer, etc. They were apparently fairly well supplied with them, of either the "matchlock" or "snaphance" (flintlock) pattern, though the planters complained to the Merchant Adventurers (in their letter of August 3, from Southampton), that they were "wanting many muskets," etc. That they had some "fowling-pieces" is shown by the fact that young Billington seems (according to Bradford) to have "shot one off in his father's cabin" aboard ship in Cape Cod harbor, and there are several other coeval mentions of them.

The arms and accoutrements (besides ordnance) of the MAY-FLOWER Pilgrims, known on the authority of Bradford and Winslow to have been brought by them, included muskets ("matchlocks"), "snaphances" (flintlocks), armor ("corslets," "cuirasses," "helmets," "bandoliers," etc.), swords, "curtlaxes" (cutlasses), "daggers," powder, "mould-shot," "match" (slow- match for guns), "flints," belts, "knapsacks," "drum," "trumpet," "manacles," "leg-irons," etc., etc. "Pistols" (brass) appear in early inventories, but their absence in the early hand-to-hand encounter at Wessagussett indicates that none were then available, or that they were not trusted. It is evident from the statement of Bradford that every one of the sixteen men who went out (under command of Standish) on the "first exploration" at Cape Cod had his "musket, sword,, and corslet;" that they relied much on their armor, and hence, doubtless, took all possible with them on the ship. They probably did not long retain its use. In the letter written to the Adventurers from Southampton, the leaders complain of "wanting many muskets, much armour, &c."

Josselyn gives' the equipment he considers necessary for each man going to New England to settle:—

"Armor compleat:—

One long piece [musket] five feet or five and a half long.
One Sword.
One bandoleer.
One belt.
Twenty pounds of powder.
Sixty pounds of shot or lead, pistol and Goose-shot."

"Another list gives an idea of 'complete armor.'"

Corselet
Breast [plate or piece].
Back [ditto].
Culet (?).
Gorget [throat-piece].

Tussis [thigh-pieces].
Head-piece "[morion skull-cap]."

Bradford states that they used their "curtlaxes" (cutlasses) to dig the frozen ground to get at the Indians' corn, "having forgotten to bring spade or mattock." "Daggers" are mentioned as used in their celebrated duel by Dotey and Leister, servants of Stephen Hopkins. Bradford narrates that on one of their exploring tours on the Cape the length of guard duty performed at night by each "relief" was determined by the inches of slow-match burned ("every one standing when his turn came while five or six inches of match was burning"), clearly indicating that they had no watches with them. The "drum" and "trumpet" are both mentioned in "Mourt's Relation" in the account given of Massasoit's reception, the latter as eliciting the especial attention of his men, and their efforts at blowing it.

The Ordnance (cannon) brought in the ship consisted (probably) of ten guns, certainly of six. Of these, two (2) were "sakers,"—guns ten feet long of 3 to 4 inches bore, weighing from fifteen to eighteen hundred pounds each; two (2) were "minions" (or "falcons"),—guns of 3 1/2 inch bore, weighing twelve hundred pounds (1200 lbs.) each; and two (2) were "bases,"—small guns of 1 1/4 inch bore, weighing some three hundred pounds (300 1bs.) each. These were mounted on "the Hill" fort or platform. It is probable that besides these were the four smallest cannon, called "patereros" (or "murderers"), which, at the time of De Rasiere's visit to Plymouth in 1627, were mounted on a platform (in front of the Governor's house), at the intersection of the two streets of the town, and commanded its several approaches. It is not likely that they were sent for after 1621, because the Adventurers were never in mood to send if asked, while Bradford, in speaking of the first alarm by the Indians, says, "This caused us to plant our great ordnance in places most convenient," leaving a possible inference that they had smaller ordnance in reserve. With this ordnance was of course a proper supply of ammunition adapted to its use. The "sakers" are said to have carried a four-pound ball, the "minions" a three-pound ball, and the "bases" a ball of a pound weight. There is not entire agreement between authorities, in regard to the size, weight, and calibre of these different classes of early ordnance, or the weight of metal thrown by them, but the above are approximate data, gathered from careful comparison of the figures given by several. There is no doubt that with this heavy ordnance and ammunition they stowed among their ballast and dunnage (as was the case in Higginson's ships), their "spare chains and anchors, chalk, bricks, sea-coal (for blacksmithing), iron, steel, lead, copper, red-lead, salt," etc.; all of which they also necessarily had, and from their bulk, character, and weight, would stow as low in the ship as might be.

That a considerable "stock of trading goods" was included in the MAYFLOWER'S lading is mentioned by at least one writer, and that this was a fact is confirmed by the records of the colonists' dealings with the Indians, and the enumeration of not a few of the goods which could have had, for the most part, no other use or value. They consisted largely of knives, bracelets (bead and metal), rings, scissors, copper-chains, beads, "blue and red trading cloth," cheap (glass) jewels ("for the ears," etc.), small mirrors, clothing (e. g. "red-cotton horseman's coats—laced," jerkins, blankets, etc.), shoes, "strong waters," pipes, tobacco, tools and hard ware (hatchets, nails, hoes, fish-hooks, etc.), rugs, twine, nets, etc., etc. A fragment of one of the heavy hoes of the ancient pattern —"found on the site of the Pilgrim trading house at Manomet "—is owned by the Pilgrim Society, and speaks volumes of the labor performed by the Pilgrims, before they had ploughs and draught- cattle, in the raising of their wonderful crops of corn. Such was the MAY-FLOWER'S burden, animate and inanimate, when—the last passenger and the last piece of freight transferred from the SPEEDWELL—her anchor "hove short," she swung with the tide in Plymouth roadstead, ready to depart at last for "the Virginia plantations."

ETEXT EDITOR'S BOOKMARKS:

Anxiety to get English clothes upon their red brethren
Forks there were none
Lanterns—only "serving to make darkness visible"
Meat was held by the napkin while being cut with the knife

Booksophile

Your Local Online Bookstore

Buy Books Online from

www.Booksophile.com

Explore our collection of books written in various languages and uncommon topics from different parts of the world, including history, art and culture, poems, autobiography and bibliographies, cooking, action & adventure, world war, fiction, science, and law.

Add to your bookshelf or gift to another lover of books - first editions of some of the most celebrated books ever published. From classic literature to bestsellers, you will find many first editions that were presumed to be out-of-print.

Free shipping globally for orders worth US$ 100.00.

Use code "Shop_10" to avail additional 10% on first order.

Visit today

www.booksophile.com

CPSIA information can be obtained
at www.ICGtesting.com
Printed in the USA
LVHW041022020323
740706LV00008B/1136

9 789356 897175